Healed

Delivered, Set Free, Restored

A 10 DAY DEVOTIONAL

Nika Collins

Copyright © 2020 Nika Collins

All rights reserved. No part of this publication may be reproduced, distributed, or transmitted in any form or by any means, including photocopying, recording, or other electronic or mechanical methods, without the prior written permission of the publisher, except in the case of brief quotations embodied in critical reviews and certain other noncommercial uses permitted by copyright law.

ISBN-978-1-951300-05-0

Liberation's Publishing LLC
West Point ~ Mississippi

Table of Contents

Introduction 5

Day 1 7

Day 2 11

Day 3 15

Day 4 21

Day 5 25

Day 6 29

Day 7 33

Day 8 37

Day 9 41

Day 10 45

Introduction

Depression is real. Anxiety is real. Mental illness is real. BUT Hope is real. Help is real. Healing is real.

You are going to be fine; you always are. Yes, you will be. Allow yourself a moment to express and display your sadness and discomfort. It will get better, but you need to also be honest and say your spirit is temporarily heavy and not have to hide it. One thing I realized is that everything always ends up working out. Sometimes even better than you can imagine. Remember this when you feel like you are being challenged the most. Believe in where you are headed. See the bigger picture. Your illness does not define you. Your strength and courage do. It is going to be okay. Just breathe. You are alive and you matter. My prayer is that someone reads this book of Devotions and decides not to give up.

Day 1

It's Okay to not be Okay

Close to eight-hundred-thousand people die due to suicide every year, which is one person every 40 seconds. There are so many people young and old that has decided that they just cannot go on. Sat in church on Sunday and yet too hopeless to make it to the next. Suicide should never be the answer. God understands you do not, he understands pain that you cannot fathom. It is ok to tell God how you feel, it is ok to cry out to God. God, I need you! My God My God Where Are You? Powerful Cry! I would get up, dress up, put my make up on, but beneath it all I was hurting, and nobody knew. They did not see my silent cries. They did not see the hurt. They did not see the pain. They did not see the bitterness. They did not see the fear. But I was literally dying inside. I did not think I was beautiful. I could be in a crowded room and still feel all alone.

Have you been wondering who you are and why God put you here? Stop living your life unaware and unsure of your purpose. Find out God's plan for your life. Make the decision right now to not only live with purpose but to live for God's purpose. Somebody's life depends on you. It is ok to not be ok; it is ok to seek help where you know that help is needed. For years I tried to control my life, I tried to fix things that were beyond my control. I tried to put band aids over my past wounds, hurts, scars, and heartaches that had inflicted me deeply. So many times, I have smiled and told people that I was fine when deep down in my soul I was broken in little tiny pieces. Pieces that only God could put together again. How many times have you ask God to show you your purpose? How many times have you said, there must be more to life than this? I have felt like this before, I started to feel empty, I started to feel like I was repeating the same routine over and over and getting nowhere. I felt like I was stuck in mud, trying to move but not going anywhere.

God continually feels sorrow when he is separated from those he loves. There is no right way to grieve and there is no set timeframe in which we must process our grief. I have endured so much, and I am sure that you have. God has not removed the pain but has allowed me to face it in different ways than when obstacles first occurred. I sleep now. I do not cry constantly. I can see how he is working in my life. But it is still there. I carry sorrow with me, but I know that he understands. He has been there. I know he hears me and that makes all the difference. If you are one of those people who are facing storms in your life right now, be still and trust in the Lord, this too shall pass, and you are going to be ok. I know takes all you have got to just be strong and it's a fight just to keep it together, I know you think that you are too far gone but hope is never lost. Hold on do not let go. Just take one step closer, put one foot in front of the other. You will get through this, just follow the light in the darkness, you are going to be ok. I know your heart is heavy from those nights but just remember that you are a fighter, you never know what tomorrow holds and you are stronger than you know.

- What is causing your fear and anxiety?
- How soon will you start to apply God's promises to your everyday life?

Isaiah 41:10 "Do not fear, for I am with you; Do not be afraid, for I am your God. I will strengthen you; surely, I will uphold you with my right hand of righteousness.

Day 2

More to Life

There is one particular phrase that I have used often in my seasons of distress , "There Has To Be More To Life Than This" Actually just the other day on my way home from a nine hour work day, I began to cry alone in my car. I felt overwhelmed with life, I was overwhelmed with coming home to the same daily routine. Cooking, doing loads of laundry, making sure that my children and husband all had a hot meal before bed. By the time I would finish I would be too tired to even eat, but I had to make sure that everyone else was good. How often do you feel like the weight of the world is just weighing down on your shoulders??? Long days, sleepless nights. I know the feeling all so well. The best part of my day is having the privilege of a long hot bubble bath just to relax the tension in my muscles, only to do it all over again the next day. I know! I know! This sucks! There must be more to life than this.

God has created so much beauty in the world, he hung the stars and the moon in the heavens and made every other creature on earth. He also formed each of us humans uniquely for his purposes. As you remember this, you cannot help but be filled with awe. The evidence of his creative power is all around us. How many times have you asked God to just show you your way? Show one the right path. O Lord point out the road for me to follow. Lead me by your truth and teach me. All day long I put my hope in you. Sometimes we are so exhausted from life and do not know what to do are where to turn. To find purpose, ask yourself: Who do you want to help? There are many ways to chip away at the same problem, and it is up to you to find out who you want to help. By figuring out the specific person or people you want to help, you can easily find your purpose.

- How often do you find yourself wondering what your purpose is on earth?
- What do you really want in life?
- Write your purpose or mission statement.

Jeremiah 29:11 "For I know the plans I have for you declares the Lord. Plans to prosper you and not to harm you, plans to give you hope and a future.

Day 3

Season of Restoration

It was amazing that my first book, 'Battle of The Mind' was just launched only a few months ago and I am already writing another one. My journey has not always been easy, but it has always been worth it, God has always been loving me, watching over me and taking care of me during life's hardships even when I was not aware of it. No pain is alike, we must all walk the journey and path that God gives, yet God promises in all pain you will rejoice, and no one will take away your joy.

From the moment Adam and Eve introduced sorrow into the world by choosing sin over God, we were plunged into a state of chaos. Jesus asked for God three times to remove the pain and sorrow he faced at the cross even though he was sinless. We all must understand that seasons change and just because you're in a dark season now, that doesn't mean that you're going to stay there. Many parts of the world have four seasons in a year. They are spring, summer, fall and winter. The weather changes, plants change too. Animals change their behavior to suit the weather.

In spring, the weather begins to get warmer, trees and plants grow new leaves. Summer is the hottest season and has long, usually sunny, days.

In the fall the weather becomes mild and leaves start falling from many types of trees. Winter is the coldest season with short days. We also have spiritual seasons. Ecclesiastes 3:1, For Everything There Is A Season. It also says that God Has Made Everything in Its Time. In a dry season God seems very distant. It is when God is quiet, and you cannot hear his voice. God seems very distant in this season. In a dry season it's good to examine your heart or unconfessed sin. Dry seasons don't last forever. Just keep the faith, keep trusting, praising and worshiping him. The rain is coming. Then there's the waiting season.

God allows waiting seasons for his glory and for our good. In your season of waiting, trust that God is pruning you. He is preparing you for the next season. Keep the faith, do not doubt God's plan and goodness, and wait with expectancy. God is listening and knows exactly where you are. Hang in there. God has not forgotten you. Next there is the busy season. This is the season when you do not feel as if you have enough time to get anything done. If you find yourself in a busy season, chase after God. The world does not rest in your hands, it rests in God's hands. Next is the Test & Trials Season. If you are going through hard times in this season and do not know why you are going through, I want to encourage you that God knows and in due time all will be revealed. Allow him to strengthen your Faith in this season. Next is Spiritual Warfare. If you are in this season just remember that God has equipped, you with all the weapons to fight in this season! If you are in this season, you are doing something right. The enemy will rage war against you. Remind yourself of the story of Job. God is in complete control, so do not be afraid. "Therefore, put on the whole armor of God, so that when the day of evil comes, you may be able to stand your ground, and after you have done everything, to stand. Stand firm then, with the belt of truth buckled around your waist, with the breastplate in place, and with your feet fitted with the readiness that comes with the gospel of peace. In addition, to all this, take up the shield of faith, with which you can extinguish all the flaming arrows of the evil one. Take the helmet of salvation and the sword of the spirit, which is the word of God." Ephesians 6:17

After this there is the Happy Season in other words this is the Season of Restoration! Of course, we all would love to live in this season forever. God has made everything beautiful in its time. I was guided by God to write my first book," Battle of The Mind." after launching that book God spoke to me in my spirit for weeks. I would constantly hear him whisper restoration. Restoration is a promise from God. When God makes a promise, he fulfils it no matter what. Not only is your restoration assured but it also brings greater things that you may have lost in the past. Certainly, this is my season of RESTORATION in Jesus name.

- God is in complete control of all seasons.
- What season would you say you are currently experiencing?

Ecclesiastics 3:11 "For everything there is a season."

Day 4

Faith Over Fear

Having faith is so important. Faith goes beyond hope. Hope lives in the mind, faith is self-rooted in the heart and spirit. Faith is just as important as the air we breathe. Going through life and all its ups and downs can certainly take a toll on us. But through all the trials and tribulations we may face, it is faith that gives us that helping hand. It guides us in the right direction allowing us to discover our purpose in life.

Everything in life is far easier when we have faith. For I know the plans I have for you, declares the Lord, plans to prosper you and not to harm you, plans to give you hope and a future. We all need pain to develop, amid opposition, amid adversity, you must be willing to fight your way through. Fight for your family, fight for your marriage, fight for your house, fight for your children, fight for your dreams and visions. When pressure is applied your character is developed.

For so long I felt empty, I felt sadness, I felt hopeless. I was easily frustrated or angered. I even started to feel misunderstood and started to avoid interactions with others. I felt drained, I felt overwhelmed. I would cry frequently for no apparent reason. I felt anxious all the time, even when there was no apparent threat or identifiable source of the tension that I was feeling. I could not focus, I struggled with remembering or maintaining focus and making decisions. Fear is designed to send you into the opposite direction of God's will for your life.

Fear/Anxiety is the devil's battleground. Guard your heart and when fear tries to creep in, cast it down. Whenever I started to feel self-doubt, insecurity, frustration, and discouragement, God reminded me to trust him. Not the world's view, not my ability, not my timeframe, not my ideas. Trust him alone. When you put hope in your own desires and abilities, you set yourself up for failure. DISAPPOINTMENTS will happen. God's word is your source and foundation. Live by it, not your feelings. As I write this devotional, we are in the middle of a pandemic that is certainly causing so much fear across this world. The bible is written for times like this.

This is a time where we should be feeding our faith. When we turn on the news, we hear that things are getting worse with this covid-19 and if we do not guard our thoughts, our thoughts will create an atmosphere of anxiety that will fill your heart. I know it seems as if things are getting worse, but God is still in control. Instead of allowing anxiety into your heart, allow faith into your heart. Throughout scripture, Jesus provides perfect example of how to respond in times of crisis. Turn your hearts to the Lord and keep praying.

- What thoughts are you hanging onto the most?

- What is weighing you down?

- Write 3 things down that you have worried about, and later found God had already worked it out in your favor.

Deuteronomy 31:8 "The Lord himself goes before you and be with you; he will never leave you nor forsake you. Do not be afraid; Do not be discouraged."

Day 5

You are Fearfully and Wonderfully Made

To walk in your truth is to fully embrace who you are. Embracing yourself as a person. Living your truth frees you from seeking validation from others. You are your own responsibility so make sure you are mentally and emotionally okay without the stress of others. You are fearfully and wonderfully made in God's sight. God created us all unique and special. God is the potter and we are the clay. He made us all perfect having our own uniqueness. You were made for a purpose.

Act towards your dreams and live out your true calling in life. Often, we forget who we are in God. We hold on to past pain, hurt and resentment from our past. The deepest wounds often come from childhood, they can affect the way we see the world, ourselves and relationships. Be careful of self talk that sounds like self-pity, victim talk, defensiveness or anger. Self talk is the silent messages that swirl around in our heads. It is powerful and shapes the way you relate to the world. When you listen to the messages, you might be surprised by the tone and the words.

The way you talk to yourself will leak into the way you are with the people close to you. Your self talk might need some redirecting. This will mean being clear and strong with yourself sometimes, comforting and tender at times. Your vulnerabilities are beautiful. Do not hide them. There are parts of all of us that are soft/ tender. They are the things that you think about at 2 am, the feelings you feel that nobody knows about. Your wounds do not have to wound you anymore. They are the proof of your resilience, your strength and your courage and now they can work hard for you. First though, you will have to shine the light on them. Stop allowing the Enemy to speak to you, stop allowing him to convince you that you are anything other than who God has created you to be.

If you cannot love you by accepting who you are, then you will never be able to fully love someone else. I'm a wife and a mother of four. I have always taught my children to love the person that God has created them to be. None of us are perfect. My husband always compliments me on how beautiful I am, but If I never believe that I am beautiful myself, I would never been able to receive those words from him. I learned that I was seeing myself through eyes of betrayal, hurt and rejection and in turn was constantly striving for approval and perfection. When I learned that these beliefs were lies authored by the world, my life was transformed. My eyes were filled with light and opened to see the truth like never before. I realized that the truth of my identity is how God sees me, but I needed to understand exactly what that was. So, I went on a journey to discover who my real identity was through the True King.

How often have you beat yourself up over past mistakes? I am sure that we all have but, God forgives, and he loves you. Of course, he does he is the one that created you. I challenge you the next time you look in the mirror to look through God's mirror, which shows us that our brokenness is made beautiful, our sins are forgiven, and by his grace, we are redeemed. You were created in God's image. God makes no mistakes. To put yourself down for the way you are is to insult God's handwork. You are beautiful.

- What is it that makes you different?
- What makes you beautiful?
- Will you embrace it all today?

2 Corinthians 5:17 "Therefore, if anyone is in Christ, he is a new creature. The old has gone the new is come."

Day 6
This Is too Big for You

A few months ago, I walked in my therapist's office with a very heavy heart. On the verge of tears, as I sit in the chair next to her, she looks me in my eyes and ask how everything had been going? Trying to answer her question without becoming an emotional mess was out the question. As soon as I started to respond the tears flowed like a river. I think I may have used the whole box of Kleenex in her office that day. I explained how I just felt so overwhelmed with life and I felt as if I had nothing else to give.

What about me? Why am I always the one giving with nothing in return, why am I always the one trying to encourage others to stay strong when I am so broken inside? I am tired, I am just so tired! I cried my eyes out in her office that day. What a blessing it is to be able to let all that frustration out to one human being and not be judged, not having to worry about her going out and putting it all out there in the streets. What a release. Therapist are a blessing. Not because I do not trust God but, sometimes we need that one person that we can just sit down with, one on one and lay it all out on the table. You would be amazed at how good it feels after leaving her office. I drove to the nail shop afterwards and spoiled myself the other half of that day.

We all have moments when we just feel as if we cannot keep going. Being a wife with four adult children who are trying to find their way, is a stressful job. My biggest problem is trying to solve all my children's problems, trying to make sure that they are doing things in the way that I feel they should be done. I struggle in the area of just letting go. Letting them find their own way.

Sure, I hate to see them taking wrong paths, but I had to find my own way, I made bad choices and I cannot control what they do when I am not around. I struggle daily letting go but I know that this issue is too big for me. I must let go and let God. I must pray and trust God to protect them in this walk. I pray daily that God strengthens me in this area. We as women wear so many hats so I know that as you read this you can totally relate. We all want what's best for our children, we don't want to see them make some of the same mistakes that we have made, we don't want to watch them take some of those same paths that we have taken but in all honesty we have to let go and let God. He holds all power in his hand. Trust him to take care of your child. Breathe. Take a moment and say this prayer. Dear God, please help me, I cannot do this on my own, I am not strong enough. I need you now and always. Please take me in your arms and hold me tight. Please protect me from this world and all this pain. Please heal my heart and soul and make me whole again. In your name amen.

- Are you trying to do it all in your own strength?
- Do not waste your weakness.
- God wants us to fully depend on him, and not ourselves.

2 Corinthians 13:9 "For we are glad when we are weak, and you are strong. Your restoration is what we pray for."

Day 7

Speak Life

How often do you speak life to those situations that seem dead in your life? My encouragement to you today is not to give up Speaking Life. Mark 11:22-24 And Jesus answered them, "Have faith in God. Truly, I say to you, whoever says to this mountain, 'Be taken up and thrown into the sea, and does not doubt in his heart, but believes that what he says will come to pass, it will be done for him. Therefore, I tell you, whatever you ask in prayer, believe that you have received it, and it will be yours. You speak life into words you say, and those words gain power and control over your life so stop saying you cannot and start saying "I WILL".

Life can make you feel that you are not getting out of life what you put in it. There are days when all we ever encounter is roadblocks, preventing us from moving forward. The moments when our dreams seem so out of reach makes us wonder if it is truly, worth fighting for. However, the challenges we face along the way are not meant to make us quit and just spend the rest of our days from the sidelines, being bitter about life. The challenges thrown in our path are meant to test us to see if we are strong enough to pass each test. It is normal to feel anxious while dealing with life and when we are pursuing our goals.

Nevertheless, that moment when you feel anxiety is the perfect occasion to keep going. Do not give up before the miracle happens. Life is not easy and there will be many situations that come your way that can cause you stress and anxiety. But no matter what your situation is right now, you must pick yourself up and stay calm and positive. The truth is this: We all have bad days. Even the most successful and happy people you see in the world want to give up. If you let fear and doubt creep in, it will start to send you in a negative, downward spiral where you will get depressed and feel like there is no hope. So, it is important that every day you feel your mind with positivity and stay strong. Be a person whose mouth is full of life. It will all depend on what is feeling your heart. Stay Positive. When you speak the word of God, you are tapping into limitless power!

- So, what will come out of your mouth today? Life or Death

Proverbs 18:21 "The tongue has the power over life and death, and those who love it will eat its fruit.

Day 8
God's Love Is Enough

John 3: 16 One of the first scriptures that I learned as a little girl was. "For God so loved the world that he gave his only begotten son, that whosoever believes in him will have everlasting life." One of my favorite songs as a little girl was, "Yes Jesus Loves ME." Amazing huh? God loves you and I just where we are. He died just so we might live. We as humans tend to love others based off how they treat us, but with God it is nothing like that. God's love for us is unconditional.

That means he loves us no matter what. God's hope is that we believe in him and accept him as our lord and savior. In doing so, we develop a personal relationship with him and will have everlasting life in heaven with him when we die. God doesn't just love a little. He loves a lot! He is full of compassion. His love is demonstrated by being patient with us, by being kind, he is fully love. God's love bears all things, hopes for all things and endures all things. For years, the enemy had me convinced that God could never forgive a sinner like me. I held on to my past, I repented and gave my life to Christ but, yet felt like my sins were too great for his forgiveness.

In my first book I mentioned how I was

convinced that my sins couldn't be forgiven, the hardest person to forgive was the one staring back at me in the mirror. Shame, Rejection, Anxious, Depressed, Sick, Weak, Addicted, Adulterous, Lonely, Failure, Mistakes, Defeated, Confused, Broken, and Hopeless. Even though we believe that Jesus sets us free, some labels are still written in what seems like permanent ink. It's a pass not easily washed away by a good thought or an encouraging word. But I'm so glad that he looked beyond all my faults and saw my needs. He certainly sees our faults, but he doesn't stop there. Our faults don't cause him to reject us but to see the deep need we have for a savior.

When I embrace God's love, my heart calms down. A quiet whisper to my soul assures me of this unconditional love. Like an anxious child soothed by the nearness of the parent, my heart rest even when the world is spinning. The love is not based on performance, on my striving to do things right, but is purely based on the truth that God loves me, no matter what. Period. And he loves you too. His arms Will open with an embrace for you. When you feel lost, lonely, discouraged, or depressed, I pray that you will remember. YOU ARE DEEPLY LOVED by God. May you be able to understand how long, how wide, how deep, and how high God's love really is. God's love reaches you wherever you are. If you are struggling with doubts about God's love, write down a few verses that reminds you of God's love, tape it to your mirror in your bathroom or bedroom and rest in God's love for you today.

- Do you ever struggle with doubts about God's love? Why?

- What lies are you believing that are causing you to doubt God's love?

- What promise from God's word can you claim today to battle these doubts?

Psalm 136:1 "Give thanks to the Lord, because He is good, His love is eternal."

Day 9
Giving Up Is Not an Option

How many times have you felt that you just couldn't go on another day? How many times have you thought about giving up? Well, I have been there, I have faced days when I did not even want to get out of bed, I did not want to face life and all the struggles that comes along with it. You need to understand that seasons change, it will not rain forever. The sun will shine again in your life. Life is not easy and there will be many situations that come your way that can cause you stress and anxiety. But no matter what your situation is right now, you must pick yourself up and stay calm and positive.

The truth is this: We all have bad days. Even the most successful people you see in the world want to give up. It is so important that every day you feed your mind with positivity. Remember, giving up is not an option. Even on those difficult days there is still hope, so keep pushing. Even if you must take a rest, get back up afterwards and push even harder. God is on your team and he will see you through. In my first book I talked about my mom and the stroke that she suffered in 2017, in the beginning it wasn't looking good at all, she wasn't able to hold her head up, she couldn't sit up, she couldn't chew any food, she couldn't even walk. But I watched God work miracles in a matter of days. I witnessed God breathe life into my mom and today she continues to fight for all that she lost. I challenge you to stay in the fight, you may get knocked off your feet, you may even get back up with scars and bruises but what matters is, YOU GOT UP!

You are stronger than you know, you will get through this just like you did the last time and the time before that. So many times the enemy had me convinced that I was in this all alone, he had me convinced that I was the only person that fell weak at times but truth is everyone struggles with something, some are just better at hiding it then others. Yes, we as women want to be the best wives to our husbands, we want to be the best mothers to our children, but truth is none of us are perfect. You will make mistakes.

Mistakes are a part of life. Stop being so hard on yourself. Do what you can, and God will do the rest. Self-criticism can take a toll on our minds and bodies. It's time to ease up on yourself. You must never give up. No matter how hard it is, no matter how much it takes out of you never give up on your dreams. Nothing is easy in life and if it is easy it is not worth it. What makes your life better are the things that you achieve after overcoming struggles or obstacles. Every obstacle you come across gives you experience that makes you stronger. One must persevere and only then will they taste the pleasure of success. It is easy to lecture people about not giving up when nobody knows what they are going through but when you think about it is not absurd because every person is going through their own struggles and problems and if they are not giving up they know that you can overcome it all too. Before you give up, think about why you held on so long.

- Are you feeling down, frustrated or low in energy, spirit?
- Take a few minutes and write down what you are grateful for.
- Focus your brain on positive thoughts.

Joshua 1:8 "Have I not commanded you, be strong and courageous. Do not be afraid, do not be discouraged, for the Lord your God will be with you wherever you go."

Day 10
God Wants to Heal You Spiritually

As I write this last entry, I hope that you have been inspired to keep holding on to God promises. I have had days when I did not even want to get out of bed, I was depressed, bitter, drained and just tired of this thing called life. But realizing that it is not always going to be this way has challenged me to keep going, so during this journey called life I will keep going and trusting God to lead every step of the way. I need you to know that if the clouds are dark in your life today it will not stay that way, the sun will shine again in your life.

I am so thankful for healing and you should be too. Healing does not mean the damage never existed. It means the damage no longer controls our lives. Everything you need, your courage, strength, compassion and love, is already within you. What is broken can be mended, what hurts can be healed, and no matter how dark it gets, the sun is going to rise again. As I reminisce over my life, all the good even the bad, I don't think that I would change a thing, the struggles that I have endured has molded me into the beautiful soul that I am today.

Pain makes you stronger, tears make you braver, and the heartbreaks make you wiser, so thank the past for a better future. God has heard your prayer and seen your tears; he will heal you. Often we get stuck focusing on all the negative in our lives, we tend to forget about all the positive, so on those days when you start to feel depression or sadness sneaking up on you, remember to just breathe and focus on all the goodness of God. Healing is available for each one of us, we just must know how to embrace the healing that God has for us.

The enemy is good at reminding us of our failures. God Healed Me, he can heal you too. I cannot see the future, but I have made the decision to follow God's lead and that meant letting the future comes as he wills it. Remember that Jesus is with you in your darkest hour. God covers you at that moment in a way that is indescribable, his grace is sufficient because he cares for you. Allow God's grace to cover you by acknowledging that your sins are not greater than his love and compassion for you, he frees you of all the guilt you carry.

Had I known the journey God would take me on when I prayed for healing, I do not think I would have had the courage to ask. But God, in his wisdom, gentleness, and love, did not take me on the entire journey overnight; instead, he asked me to trust him for just the step-in front of me. He led me slowly, patiently, giving me space to grieve, rage, and grow. He provided everything I needed to experience the healing he offers, and he will do the same for you. God is not just the one that healed in the bible days. Jesus is the same yesterday, and today, and forever. Keep your words in line with God's promises each and every day. God's Word, taken daily like medicine, is health to your spirit, soul and body!

- Do you need God's healing in an area of your life?

- Write down 3 ways you will stay focused on your healing process?

Psalm 147:3 "He health the broken heart, and bindeth up their wounds.

www.ingramcontent.com/pod-product-compliance
Lightning Source LLC
Chambersburg PA
CBHW052106110526
44591CB00013B/2377